Dinosaurs

KINGFISHER

KINGFISHER

First published 2012 by Kingfisher
an imprint of Macmillan Children's Books
a division of Macmillan Publishers Limited
20 New Wharf Road, London N1 9RR
Basingstoke and Oxford
Associated companies throughout the world
www.panmacmillan.com

ISBN 978-0-7534-3251-8

Consultant: Dr Darren Naish

Designed and created by Basher www.basherbooks.com
Text written by Dan Green

Dedicated to Ellen and Tommy Southgate

Text and design copyright © Toucan Books Ltd 2012
Based on an original concept by Toucan Books Ltd
Illustrations copyright © Simon Basher 2012

9 8 7 6 5 4 3 2 1
1TR/0512/AYL/WKT/140MA

A CIP catalogue record for this book
is available from the British Library.

Printed in China

Note to readers: the website addresses listed above are correct at the time
of going to print. However, due to the ever-changing nature of the internet,
website addresses and content can change. Websites can contain links that
are unsuitable for children. The publisher cannot be held responsible for changes
in website addresses or content, or for information obtained through a third party.
We strongly advise that internet searches should be supervised by an adult.

CONTENTS

Introduction
Dinosaurs

The world has seen *nothing* quite like the dinosaurs. From terrifying T. rex to massive Argentinosaurus, these stupendous, ancient beasts thrived for 160 million years – the largest animals ever to have lived. A man called Richard Owen (1804–92) gave dinosaurs their name. Literally, it means "terrible lizard". But really! Prehistoric giants? Ever feel like someone is pulling your leg?

Well, think again! It may bust your brainbox, but there is hard evidence for the things we know about dinosaurs. Scientists called palaeontologists find dino bones in rocks that are millions of years old. These remains give clues to an animal's lifestyle: teeth that shred leaves look very different to those that bite chunks of flesh or crack open shells. Hips tell us which group of dinosaurs a skeleton fits into: saurischians (saw-isk-ee-ans) with "lizard hips" or ornithiscians (orn-ee-thisk-ee-ans) with "bird hips". It's taken well over a hundred years to figure out that our planet is always changing and, as it does, life evolves and adapts to the new conditions. Get ready – you're about to see some of the most weird, but utterly real creatures!

Palaeontologists

Chapter 1
Vege-munchers

Size, when you're a plant-eater, really matters! You've not met the Meat-crunchers yet, but you will soon see that they are not a nice bunch. Sure, some of the Vege-munchers were blessed with spiked tails and armoured plates, but not all of them. Quite often their only other defence was to pack on the pounds. Boy, did these guys guzzle the greenery! They were a gassy bunch, too. Well, imagine: tough Jurassic plant matter, eaten in vast quantities, digested in gigantic pot bellies filled with super-strong acid. Mmm, if you're still interested in meeting this lot, you'd better stay downwind!

Iguanodon

Brachiosaurus

Maiasaura

Triceratops

Stegosaurus

Parasaurolophus

Ankylosaurus

Pachyceph-
alosaurus

Diplodocus

Argentinosaurus

Iguanodon
Vege-munchers

* A herding herbivore with a handy set of back gnashers
* Had a "fifth finger" on each forelimb for grasping vegetation
* This plant-lover inhabited most of Europe

I am a dino diva – literally one of the very first dinosaurs to be named (get me!). My skeletons have been found all over Europe and have given scientists plenty to think about when it comes to my appearance and lifestyle.

A strict vegetarian, my toothless beak has an overbite that is very handy for cropping tough foliage. I like to chew well and have perfected the art of slice-'n'-dice feeding. Using around one hundred, tightly packed back teeth, I literally shred my food to bits before swallowing. Hooves on my forelimbs show that I walk on all fours, but I can stand on two to feed from high branches. Like all plant-eaters, I'm easy prey but, behold, a secret weapon: spiked thumbs that are perfect for jabbing at bullies. Not quite the thumbs-up a predator looks for!

- Discovered: 1822 (UK)
- Pronounced: ig-wha-noh-don
- Name means: iguana tooth
- Period: Early Cretaceous
- Lived: 126–125 million years ago
- Size: up to 10 m long; 5 tonnes

Iguanodon

Brachiosaurus
 Vege-munchers

※ A dino with a small head, a short tail and a long, long neck
※ Reached plants that no others could… and scoffed the lot!
※ This biggy lived exclusively in North America

I'm no great risk-taker, but I do like to stick my neck out once in a while. Just look at it – towering a ludicrous nine metres above my body, it's not as if I have much choice!

Scientists believe I must have a huge heart to pump blood all that way. What can I say? I'm a big-hearted kinda guy! Just as well, 'cos I'm not big on brain – with a neck this long, the last thing you need is a heavy head to support. With front legs that are longer than my back legs and a short tail, I'm a high-browser, able to reach foliage at great heights for my nourishment. Of course, I can swing low to eat, too… if I want to. My fossils have left scientists guessing at my size, but at more than a tonne a metre, I have to eat like there's no tomorrow. You gotta love the green stuff, I can tell you!

● Discovered: 1900 (Colorado, USA)
● Pronounced: brak-ee-oh-sore-us
● Name means: arm lizard

● Period: Late Jurassic
● Lived: 154–153 million years ago
● Size: up to 23 m long; 40 tonnes

Brachiosaurus

Maiasaura

■ Vege-munchers

❋ This mumsy duck-billed beast could go on two legs or four
❋ A social animal that laid its eggs in communal nesting sites
❋ Thought to have inhabited just North America

Hello my dear, you can call me Ducky! I tend to hang out with my own kind, so it's very important for me to get along with folk. Sometimes there are thousands of us in a single herd – handy for keeping Meat-crunchers at bay!

My duck-billed sisters and I make our nests beside each other in a great nursery. What better way to create a nurturing environment in which to raise the little ones and keep them safe from harm? I take great care of my eggs, covering them with rotten plants to make sure they stay hidden and warm. Like my vege-munching cousin, Iguanodon, I have no front teeth, but my back teeth are arranged in batteries (that's lots of them jammed in tight) for slicing and dicing. Whenever one tooth wears out, a fresh one is always primed, ready to go. Chomp!

● Discovered: 1978 (Montana, USA)
● Pronounced: my-ah-sore-ah
● Name means: good mother lizard
● Period: Late Cretaceous
● Lived: 74 million years ago
● Size: up to 9 m long; 2.5 tonnes

Maiasaura

Triceratops
Vege-munchers

* A bulldozer with a super-large skull
* Safe from most predators once grown to full size
* A common beast, yet only inhabited North America

I'm a rootin' tootin' good old boy. I've got a barrel belly and a bad temper to boot. I don't wish harm to others, I just don't dig hassle. I'm a six-tonne juggernaut and I'll stand my ground. And if there's any doubt... I'll charge!

Hey, I'm no looker, but my half-tonne head certainly catches the eye. With three great horns and a frill that's six times thicker than a human skull, woe betide anything that encounters my business end. The frill shields the vulnerable parts of my neck, but I also use it to flash and wink at pretty young things. I spend my time roaming the plains and forests, cropping vegetation with my bony beak. Many of my fossils bear evidence of fierce encounters with power-crazy Tyrannosaurus rex, but healed scars on my frill show that I don't give up easily.

- Discovered: 1887 (Colorado, USA)
- Pronounced: tri-serra-tops
- Name means: three-horned face
- Period: Late Cretaceous
- Lived: 68–65 million years ago
- Size: up to 9 m long; 6 tonnes

Triceratops

Stegosaurus
Vege-munchers

* The bus-sized dino with bony plates on its back
* This heavy-metal Jurassic giant was well protected
* Inhabited western North America and Europe

Talk about armour – I've got hip guards, neck studs and 17 pairs of diamond-shaped bony plates running down my back. These deter the baddies, while the wicked spikes in my tail deal with those daft enough to strike.

Swung from side to side, my thagomizer (that's the spiked tail) pulverizes anything that tries to sneak up on me or get around my rear end. Ouch! It's no surprise that most Meat-crunchers leave me alone once I'm fully grown. Although used mostly for display, science bods think my plates may also have played a secondary role in temperature control. Sounds wacky, eh? The idea is that the honeycomb of blood vessels pumps blood into the plates to help me cool off when I'm hot and bothered or to absorb heat when I'm feeling chilly. *Brrr*!

- Discovered: 1877 (Colorado, USA)
- Pronounced: steg-oh-sore-us
- Name means: roof lizard
- Period: Late Jurassic
- Lived: 155–150 million years ago
- Size: up to 9 m long; 4 tonnes

Stegosaurus

Parasaurolophus
Vege-munchers

* Smooth soul brother with a built-in hooter and a big brain
* A slow-chewing plant-grinder who lived as part of a herd
* This crest-headed wonder inhabited North America

I'm a cool cat, man, a totally groovesome jazz-o-saurus. That's right, my friend – my hooter is a tooter. My nasal cavity doubles back on itself inside the 1.8-metre, backward-pointing crest that sits right up on top of my noodle. C'mon, don't pretend you haven't seen it!

My amazing conk is connected to my throat and when I make a sound it resonates in the bone chambers like a super-low-frequency foghorn. I can communicate over long distances, keeping the herd together or barking out alarm calls to warn of danger. Like my bug-eyed pal, Iguanodon, I go about on all fours, but rear up on two legs for noshing on high branches. I have four batteries of rear gnashers – around 800 teeth in total. Locked tight together, they form a single, foliage-grinding megatooth.

- Discovered: 1922 (Alberta, Canada)
- Pronounced: pa-ra-sore-rol-off-us
- Name means: near-crested lizard
- Period: Late Cretaceous
- Lived: 76.5–73 million years ago
- Size: up to 11 m long; 2.5 tonnes

Parasaurolophus

Ankylosaurus

■ Vege-munchers

※ A slow-moving, blunderbuss herbivore that liked to be alone
※ Despite its armour, no complete skeleton has been found
※ This thick-skinned dino inhabited western North America

I go about on stout legs, keeping my head low as I chomp on grasses and shrubbery. But – bish bash bosh – I'm one big bully boy, bristling with armoured plates and knobs of bone. A massive club sits at the end of my chunky tail. With huge muscles to sweep it from side to side, it pounds and pummels attackers, breaking bones with each swing. Predators, beware!

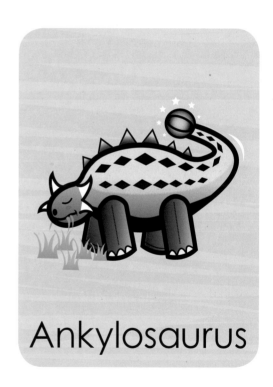

Ankylosaurus

- Discovered: 1908 (Montana, USA)
- Pronounced: an-kie-loh-sore-us
- Name means: fused lizard

- Period: Late Cretaceous
- Lived: 66.5–65.5 million years ago
- Size: up to 7 m long; 6 tonnes

Pachycephalosaurus

Vege-munchers

- Dome-headed dinosaur and potential headbutter
- Enjoyed a mixed diet of leaves, seeds and fruit
- Thick skull fossils have been found in North America alone

Pachyceph-alosaurus

Hey! You wouldn't wanna crack heads with me, I can tell you. Donk! See, no pain. Thwack! No dizziness. My head is capped with a 25-cm-thick bony dome (leaving precious little room for a brain). I also sport some pretty rad nose cones and spikes around the back of my neck. I run on two legs and use my sharp nipping teeth to tear and taste all sorts of veggie treats. Yum!

- Discovered: 1859 (Montana, USA)
- Pronounced: pack-i-kef-al-oh-sore-us
- Name means: thick-headed lizard
- Period: Late Cretaceous
- Lived: 70–65.5 million years ago
- Size: up to 4.5 m long; 0.45 tonnes

Diplodocus
Vege-munchers

* The longest dinosaur known from a complete skeleton
* Recently found to have had a row of spines down its back
* A peg-toothed dino that inhabited North America

Hey brother! If you want to walk with dinosaurs, join my laid-back vege-munching crew. When you get this long, there's not much that troubles you apart from finding food... if you happen to trough a tonne of plants a day!

My impressively long neck is handy for poking about low branches and the shrubbery. I just love a tasty fern, and will bulldoze swathes of forest to get to it. I have been known to topple trees with my tremendous bulk! Visually, my neck is elegantly counterbalanced by my equally long bullwhip tail. Packed with muscle, I can power the tip to swat at unwanted guests. Jurassic veggies have their merits but, in the quantities I get through, it's not all rosy. Bacteria in my gut break down and ferment the food, producing gloriously whiffy farts! Just imagine...

- Discovered: 1877 (Colorado, USA)
- Pronounced: di-plod-oh-kuss
- Name means: double beam
- Period: Late Jurassic
- Lived: 154–150 million years ago
- Size: up to 26 m long; 12 tonnes

Diplodocus

Argentinosaurus
Vege-munchers

* This hunka-chunka dino is one of the largest ever discovered
* A monster plant-eater supported by ma-hoo-ssive bones
* Not many bones of this beast have been discovered

Ka-*boom*! I'm the South American super heavyweight, one of the largest land animals that the Earth has ever known. As an adult, I stand as tall as a five-storey building and as long as three school buses. My footprints alone can be deathtraps for smaller animals.

Possibly the heaviest dinosaur of all time, I'm 41 tonnes meat, 16 tonnes fat, 11 tonnes bone, 4 tonnes blood and 3 tonnes hide. Wowzer! Baby Argies weigh just a few kilos, which means they need to do some serious gobbling of their greens to grow to my great size (it'll take 'em about 40 years). Good job our toothy-pegs are well adapted for a lifetime of guzzling – there's simply no time to chew when you have to pack on the pounds. These little nippers can strip a branch of foliage in one sweep!

- Discovered: 1993 (Argentina)
- Pronounced: ar-jent-eeno-sore-us
- Name means: Argentina lizard
- Period: Late Cretaceous
- Lived: 95 million years ago
- Size: up to 30 m long; 75 tonnes

Argentinosaurus

Chapter 2
Meat-crunchers

Everybody loves a bad guy and these nasties are no exception. Clawed and jawed, with feathered or scaly skin and mouths brimming with pointy teeth, they have a reputation for violence that is every bit as scary today as it was 100 million years ago. Outnumbered by the Vege-munchers, the Meat-crunchers left an *impression* nonetheless, evolving in tandem with their veggie prey. For every massive plant-lover there was also a giant meat-shredder. Several of these beasts hunted in packs and some of them were pretty fast. So you'd better watch out for what's hiding in the bushes as you step this way…

Coelophysis

Tyrannosaurus rex

Allosaurus

Oviraptor

Spinosaurus

Baryonyx

Deinonychus

Velociraptor

Coelophysis
■ Meat-crunchers

☀ This diddy tyke was one of the first theropod dinosaurs
☀ May have hunted in packs to prey on larger beasts
☀ A little nipper that has been found all over the world

Lithe and speedy, I am a titch compared to the monster meat-shredding dinos that followed me. But what does size matter when you're an evolutionary marvel?

That's right! I have a smart pair of slinky lizard-hips, which allow my legs to drop directly beneath my body. With this solid support, I can stand more upright than many of the creatures from the previous 30 million years. Just watch me scamper about on two legs, while using my strong front limbs to grab things. What's that? Anyone can do it? Well, that's easy for you to say 210 million years later, but it was totally revolutionary in my day. And what's more, my skull has large windows in it and the bones of my limbs are hollow, keeping me lightweight and nimble. And you? Mmm, not so clever now, eh?

● Discovered: 1881 (New Mexico, USA)
● Pronunciation: seel-oh-fie-sis
● Name means: hollow form
● Period: Late Triassic
● Lived: 216.5–203.5 million years ago
● Size: up to 3 m long; 30 kg

Coelophysis

Tyrannosaurus rex
■ Meat-crunchers

✳ A towering terror with tiny arms and a bone-crunching bite
✳ With a long stride, T. rex could run at around 40 km/h
✳ This meanie tyrannized western North America

Rooaaaarrrrr! You should be shakin' in your shoes and a-quakin' at the thought of me, Tyrant King of dinosaurs. Trust me, if it walks, it's dinner – I'll even eat my own kind.

I'm a seek-and-destroy powerhouse. My forward-pointing peepers give me hawk-eye vision, and whopping smell centres let me sniff out fresh meat and carrion over great distances. Despite my weight, I can be surprisingly light on my feet, allowing me to sneak up on my prey if I want to. My massive skull is kitted out with flesh-shredding, saw-edged teeth, while powerful muscles in my neck help me to pull and tear an animal to pieces once I've sunk my slashing gnashers in. You can see how well built I am, and yet my puny front limbs seem a joke. Honestly, I can barely scratch my chin. Go on, laugh, I dare you!

● Discovered: 1902 (Montana, USA)
● Pronunciation: tie-ran-oh-sore-us rex
● Name means: tyrant lizard king
● Period: Late Cretaceous
● Lived: 67–65 million years ago
● Size: up to 12 m long; 6 tonnes

Tyrannosaurus rex

Allosaurus
■ Meat-crunchers

✳ Ruthless killer with evil-looking ridge crests on the nose
✳ A common predator; possibly hunted in packs
✳ Fossils found in North America and Europe

Boy, oh boy, do I love surprises! Sadly, peaceful plant-nibblers like Stegosaurus and Camptosaurus don't agree! I'm an ambush hunter. I creep up on other animals and then – Boo! – I burst from cover and run them down.

Sleek and slimline, I'm no lumberer. I can shift it over short distances, running at 30 to 50 km/h. With a set of kitchen knives in my mouth – truly vicious, saw-edged teeth – I can take out chunks of flesh while on the run. With my prey cornered, I jack my jaw wide open like a bear trap and sink my top row of pearly whites in, chopping like a hatchet. The damage this does to meat and muscle is staggering. And should anyone dare to struggle, I hold them close in my strong arms until the wriggling stops... it's "Allo" from me and goodbye from them!

- Discovered: 1877 (Colorado, USA)
- Pronunciation: al-oh-sore-us
- Name means: different lizard
- Period: Late Jurassic
- Lived: 155–145 million years ago
- Size: up to 8 m long; 2 tonnes

Allosaurus

Oviraptor
■ Meat-crunchers

✴ This little critter is an egg-snatching, Mongolian mystery
✴ A toothless wonder with feathered arms but no wings
✴ Known from just one official fossil, found in the Gobi Desert

Who's a pretty boy then? Kwawk! I'm a prehistoric Polly, a dinosaur with a parrot beak. Some scientists think I'm more bird than dino, but I can assure you, I'm no turkey!

When my bones were found on top of a nest full of eggs, dino-diggers figured I had been caught stealing and they named me "egg thief". But the "yolk" was on them, 'cos I was busy minding my own! I don't have any teeth, so it might seem odd that I'm a meat-eater, and I have baffled scientists in the past. However, recent discoveries have revealed more about my eating habits – that I eat plants as well as tasty sauropodlet snacks, for example, which makes me something of an omnivore. My short, powerful beak could also be pretty handy for cracking open a few eggs! I like 'em fresh in the morning!

● Discovered: 1923 (Mongolia)
● Pronunciation: oh-vee-rap-tor
● Name means: egg thief

● Period: Late Cretaceous
● Lived: 75 million years ago
● Size: up to 2 m long; 25 kg

Oviraptor

Spinosaurus
■ Meat-crunchers

❊ Sail-backed dino with a crocodile face and fishy breath
❊ The last and largest of the fish-eating dinosaurs (piscivores)
❊ Hung out in the forest swamps of North Africa

I am the Cretaceous colossus, the biggest killer to bash about on dry land. T. rex? Why, that puny patsy wouldn't even dare to look me in the eye!

I can hunt down and tear apart any animal, sure, but it's fish I really love – gimme bus-sized sawfish. My long snout has nostrils placed high up, allowing me to trail my pressure-sensitive nose in the water. I can literally feel my prey approaching and strike without seeing it. Instead of the jagged-edged teeth of other Meat-crunchers, mine are smooth and bullet-shaped – ideal for stabbing and grabbing. Three razor-sharp claws on my hands do the rest! I am the top predator in these climes, but my position is fragile. Rising sea levels will eventually wipe out the swamplands where I live and I'll be hung out to dry!

● Discovered: 1912 (Egypt)
● Pronunciation: spine-oh-sore-us
● Name means: thorn lizard

● Period: Early/Late Cretaceous
● Lived: 112–97 million years ago
● Size: up to 14 m long; 10 tonnes

Spinosaurus

Baryonyx
■ Meat-crunchers

✸ Crocodile-snouted fish guzzler and relative of Spinosaurus
✸ Had a massive hooked claw on each hand
✸ This piscivore hunted in rivers in western Europe

I have a smile you won't forget easily! My mouth bristles with small, serrated teeth – 96 in all. That's twice as many as T. rex, and three times as many as you. Say cheese!

Like Spinosaurus, I'm a fish-eater and I like to hang out along riverbanks and marshes. My slender snout stretches all the way to a delicate, thin tip with a scooped end. My conical teeth have very fine sawlike edges – just the thing for snagging passing fishies and holding on to their wriggling bodies. Snappy! I'm also kitted out with my very own gaffs (that's fishing hooks to you), two half-metre-long hooked claws that make landing large fish a cinch. If you go to Alaska today, you'll see grizzly bears using the same method to spear salmon in the rapids. With claws like these, fish "bearly" stand a chance. Ha!

● Discovered: 1983 (Surrey, UK)
● Pronunciation: bah-ree-on-icks
● Name means: heavy claw

● Period: Early Cretaceous
● Lived: 130–125 million years ago
● Size: up to 9.5 m long; 2.5 tonnes

Baryonyx

Deinonychus
■ Meat-crunchers

☀ Brainy birdlike dinosaur that may have had feathers
☀ Nimble and lightly built; used its tail for balance
☀ This relative of Velociraptor lived in western North America

Speedy and agile, I have grasping fingers with long, curving claws. My mouth is full of sharp slashing teeth, designed to rip out chunks of flesh. Think that's scary? Well, think again. See the sickle-shaped second toe of each foot? Those are my daggers of death. Held off the ground when I run, they come down like blades when I leap onto my prey, gouging, tearing and mangling. Shudder!

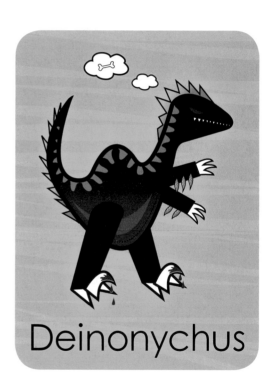

Deinonychus

● Discovered: 1964 (Montana, USA)
● Pronunciation: die-non-i-kuss
● Name means: terrible claw

● Period: Early Cretaceous
● Lived: 115–108 million years ago
● Size: up to 3.5 m long; 60 kg

Velociraptor
Meat-crunchers ∎

* A big-brained, turkey-sized scavenger
* Fossilized in mortal combat with herbivore Protoceratops
* This violent critter roamed the wilds of Mongolia in Asia

Velociraptor

With my narrow head and long, feathered forelimbs I am a curious-looking beast, I know. But looks aren't everything! The ultimate dino villain, I'm bloodthirsty and out for the kill. I have a mean-grip jaw, killer claws and a tendency to go for the jugular. Speed is always of the essence and my stiff tail stops me from teetering when in hot pursuit of a tasty snack.

- Discovered: 1923 (Mongolia)
- Pronunciation: vel-oss-ee-rap-tor
- Name means: speedy thief

- Period: Late Cretaceous
- Lived: 75–71 million years ago
- Size: up 2.5 m long; 25 kg

Chapter 3
High-flyers

Strap on your flying goggles and prepare to take to the air with this brood of blue-sky riders. Aviation enthusiasts one and all, the High-flyers are recognized as the world's first flying vertebrates (animals with backbones to you). Not all of these critters were dinosaurs. Pterodactylus and Quetzalcoatlus were specialist reptiles with hollow bones and large brains to control their flight. Members of the dromaeosaur family of dinosaurs, Rahonavis and Microraptor can claim to be true ancestors of the birds we see today. They were the first to grow feathers for show, for keeping warm and even for flight.

Pterodactylus

Quetzalcoatlus

Rahonavis

Microraptor

Archaeopteryx

Pterodactylus
High-flyers

* Furry flying reptile with a coloured crest and pouchy throat
* Armed with clawed fingers, a pointy beak and sharp teeth
* This non-dino has left its traces across Europe

A-duckin' and a-divin', a-skimmin' and a-bobbin', I love to fly the Jurassic skies. Each of my leathery wings hangs from an incredibly long fourth finger and stretches all the way to the ankle. I'm an airborne wonder. Tally ho!

Some people think I am a dinosaur, but actually I'm a very close relative. My turbocharged breast muscles provide all a chap needs for powering flight, sometimes over long distances. My sharp little brain is capable of calculating fantastic tucks and bends, and a short tail allows me to make some stunning in-flight manoeuvres. But I don't always have my head in the clouds. Nope, when it comes to food, you'll see me wading along the shoreline looking for crustaceans and molluscs. Armed with pin-sharp teeth, resistance is futile. Crunch!

- Discovered: 1780 (Germany)
- Pronunciation: ter-oh-dak-til-us
- Name means: winged finger
- Period: Late Jurassic
- Lived: 150–148 million years ago
- Size: up to 1.5m wingspan; 4.5 kg

Pterodactylus

Quetzalcoatlus
High-flyers

- Cruising bruiser with a wingspan the size of a light aircraft
- The largest flying beast ever to have existed on Earth
- This terror of the skies inhabited North America

I'm an easy rider. With very little effort, I catch rising warm air under my leathery folds of skin to rise up, up, up where I can survey vast areas of the plains. Soaring high above the Earth, I use my impressive wings to keep me afloat and my beady eyes peeled for juicy snacks.

Everything about me is huge. It would take a champion long jumper to leap from one end of my head to the other. Fully opened, my wings stretch wider than a tennis court and are suspended from a fourth finger that could match the height of a football goalpost. When I land, I stand almost as tall as a giraffe. Stumping about on all fours, I hunt small reptiles and sauropodlets, bringing my great pointed beak stabbing down on them. I also like to jab about in the odd rotting carcass. Finders, keepers!

- Discovered: 1972 (Texas, USA)
- Pronunciation: kwet-zal-co-at-lus
- Name means: feathered serpent
- Period: Late Cretaceous
- Lived: 68–65.5 million years ago
- Size: up to 12 m wingspan; 250 kg

Quetzalcoatlus

Rahonavis
 High-flyers

- ✳ Raven-sized dino-bird and relative of the dromaeosaurs
- ✳ Like all dromaeosaurs, this dino had a raised sickle claw
- ✳ Hailed from the African island of Madagascar

I'm a diddy little feathered fella, a speedy runner and a darting predator. At some point in time, millions of years ago, modern birds evolved from dinos just like me. Experts think I might have taken to the skies, too. Well, look at my long, muscly arms. Why shouldn't they support wings that I can flap to get me airborne? Hence my reputation, I say, as a menace from the clouds.

Rahonavis

- ● Discovered: 1995 (Madagascar)
- ● Pronunciation: rah-hoo-nay-vis
- ● Name means: menace bird
- ● Period: Late Cretaceous
- ● Lived: 70 million years ago
- ● Size: up to 70 cm long; 1 kg

Microraptor
High-flyers

* Mini gliding dino-bird with four wings and a long tail
* A poor ground-runner, this critter lived in the trees
* Most common dromaeosaur fossil, many with plumage

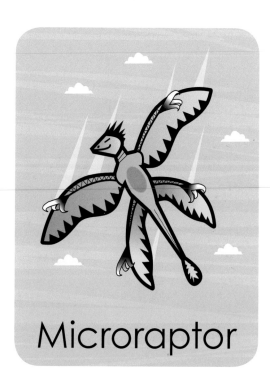

Microraptor

Hey! Up here! Watch me skitter about in the trees, digging my claws in for the climb. Admiring my fabulous feathers? You should be, 'cos these fancy things are not for warmth or colourful display. No, I use these bad boys for flight while my long, stabilizing tail guides my descent. Swooping and gliding back down to Earth, you could say I'm a dino*soar*!

* Discovered: 2003 (China)
* Pronunciation: mike-row-rap-tor
* Name means: small thief

* Period: Early Cretaceous
* Lived: 120 million years ago
* Size: up to 40 cm long; 1 kg

Archaeopteryx
High-flyers

* This dino-bird's discovery supported the theory of evolution
* One of the earliest birds, but still counted as a dinosaur
* This handsome beast inhabited Germany

I don't like to boast, but my discovery over 150 years ago takes some beating, I can tell you. At the time, I could claim to be the world's first-ever bird. Just imagine! Even though this is now disputed, my significance for the evolution of birds from dinosaurs is no less diminished.

You see, I'm definitely a dino: like my dromaeosaur relatives, I have small biting teeth in my beak, clawed fingers in my wing, a cocked "killing claw" and a long bony tail. But (and it's a big but) like modern birds, I also have flight-ready feathers. If you don't believe me, look at my exquisite fossils. These glorious impressions made in the mud were found just two years after Charles Darwin published his theories on evolution. I helped to prove that he really had something. Boy, he must have loved me!

- Discovered: 1861 (Germany)
- Pronunciation: ark-ee-op-ter-ix
- Name means: ancient wing

- Period: Late Jurassic
- Lived: 150–148.5 million years ago
- Size: up to 50 cm long; 1 kg

Archaeopteryx

Chapter 4
Water Lovers

Here's a fine bunch of scary sea monsters, huge predatory beasts that prowled the world's oceans with menace. Around at the same time as the dinos that roamed the land, these fearsome Water Lovers actually belonged to a group of marine reptiles. Like modern ocean-going mammals – whales, dolphins and porpoises – they were air-breathers, which means they needed to surface from time to time. These days, the only surviving marine reptiles are turtles, snakes, iguanas and crocodiles... and none are as monstrous as this lot were! Are you ready to take the plunge?

Ichthyosaurus

Liopleurodon

Plesiosaurus

Ichthyosaurus
Water Lovers

* Shark-tailed, tuna-fish-shaped marine reptile
* Warm-blooded; gave birth to live young in the water
* This swift-swimmer has left its mark in Europe

Whoosh! Streamlined and slick, I'm built for sheer speed in the water. See me flashing past, and I bet you'd be forced to look twice. You might think that I'm a huge tuna, but I'm no fish – I'm reptile to the bone!

I power myself along using my tail, sweeping it graciously from side to side like a shark. I have stiff fins that help me manoeuvre, twist and tumble in the water. And I tuck them in tight to my body when I need a burst of speed. My top-mounted dorsal fin gives me stability as I swim and a nice "ride" in the water. I am an air-breather, like a dolphin, and my big eyes show that I am an active chaser of fish. I have lovely pointed teeth – perfect for cracking open shellfish ammonites or crunchy, squiddy belemnites. Mmm, nice with a squeeze of lemon!

- Discovered: 1811 (UK)
- Pronunciation: ick-thee-oh-sore-us
- Name means: fish lizard
- Period: Late Triassic/Early Jurassic
- Lived: 200–185 million years ago
- Size: up to 2 m long; 90 kg

Ichthyosaurus

Liopleurodon
Water Lovers

✳ Gigantic, powerfully built, short-necked shark eater
✳ Predator of the Jurassic seas; Earth's largest carnivore… ever
✳ Fossils of this massive beast have been found in Europe

Behold, the top terror of the Jurassic seas, master of the largest jaws this planet has ever seen! A monster mega-predator, I'll have large fry for supper. My huge teeth make short work of bones and gristle. Chomp!

Considered antisocial and violent, when I say "come round for dinner" it's not exactly a chat over a light bite that I'm after. I cruise underwater, moving slowly and menacingly. I have a large, compact head and an impressively muscular body and tail. Flapping my front and back fins out of time with each other, what I lack in grace, I make up for in power. I'm an ambush killer – my giant flippers give me blistering acceleration on demand. I hunt using my sharp sense of smell, sweeping my head from side to side, silently searching. Sniff, sniff!

● Discovered: 1873 (France)
● Pronunciation: lie-oh-plew-roh-don
● Name means: smooth-sided teeth
● Period: Mid/Late Jurassic
● Lived: 162–150 million years ago
● Size: up to 15 m long; 20 tonnes

Liopleurodon

Plesiosaurus
Water Lovers

* Marine reptile with a short tail, a long neck and four flippers
* Able to swim faster than an Olympic swimmer
* This underwater wonder inhabited European waters

Hello there! With my toothy grin and my snappy style, I'm one happy swimmer – a fish-chasin', air-breathin', fully ocean-goin' reptile. Very "plesio" to meet you!

My body is short, broad and well muscled. They say I look like a snake threaded through a turtle shell, but that's silly 'cos I haven't even got a shell! It's true that my neck is long, but it's not that flexible. Rather, it's the expert way in which I operate my flippers that gives me the skill required for such fine swimming. I move nothing like a turtle, which only uses its front flippers for propulsion. No, I use all four: first the front pair, then the back. With a little gentle flapping, I glide through the water in pursuit of deliciously fishy food. I might even graze the ocean floor for a clam or snail. I'm a refined sort of chap, you know!

- Discovered: 1823 (UK)
- Pronunciation: pleez-ee-oh-sore-us
- Name means: ribbon lizard
- Period: Early Jurassic
- Lived: 199–176 million years ago
- Size: up to 3.5 m long; 500 kg

Plesiosaurus

Index

Character entries are **bold**

LMN

Liopleurodon **56**
Maiasaura **12**
meat-crunchers, see
  carnivores
Microraptor 42, **49**
necks 10, 14 , 21, 22, 30,
  56, 58, 63, 64
nests 12, 34, 62

O

omnivores 34, 63
ornithiscians 4, 63
Oviraptor **34**
Owen, Richard 4

PQ

Pachycephalosaurus **21**
pack-hunters 28, 32
Parasaurolophus **18**
piscivores 36, 38, 44, 54, 56,
  58, 62, 63
plant-eaters, see herbivores
Plesiosaurus **58**
Protoceratops 41
Pterodactylus 42, **44**
Quetzalcoatlus 42, **46**

RS

Rahonavis 42, **48**
reptiles 42, 44, 46, 52, 54,
  58, 62, 63, 64
saurischians 4, 64
sauropods 34, 46, 64
snouts 36, 38
Spinosaurus **36**, 38
Stegosaurus **16**, 32

T

tails 10, 16, 20, 22, 40, 41, 44,
  49, 50, 54, 56, 58, 64
tail spikes 6, 16, 64
teeth 4, 8, 12, 18, 21, 22, 24,
  26, 30, 32, 34, 36, 38, 40, 44,
  50, 54, 56, 58, 62, 63, 64
theropods 28, 64
Triassic period 28, 54, 64
Triceratops **14**
Tyrannosaurus rex 4, 14, **30**,
  36, 38, 64

VW

Velociraptor 40, **41**
wings 44, 46, 48, 49, 50

Glossary

Ammonite Belongs to an extinct group of molluscs with spiral shells. Closely related to octopus, squid and cuttlefish, but looks more like the modern nautilus. Died out at the same time as the dinosaurs.

Battery (dental) A large block of fused teeth that often have as many as five individual teeth stacked on top of each other in every position. Useful for grinding and crushing plants, and also seen in modern elephants.

Belemnite An extinct set of squidlike molluscs with a bullet-shaped, hard, internal skeleton. Became extinct around the same time as the dinosaurs.

Bipedal Walking on two legs.

Carnivore A meat-eating animal.

Carrion The body of a dead animal, also known as a "carcass". It is a food source for other animals.

Ceratopsian A herbivorous, quadrupedal, beaked dinosaur of the Cretaceous period.

Communal nesting Often seen in ceratopsian dinosaurs, as well as modern reptiles and birds, where groups of mothers lay their eggs in the same location, most probably for protection against predators. Fossilized sites give clues to dinosaur behaviour.

Crest A ridge, whirl or tube of bone on top of the head. Hadrosaur crests were often hollow and may have been used to make sounds.

Cretaceous A geological period following the Jurassic and running from 145 to 65 million years ago. During this period the climate was warm and the sea level high. This was the last age of the dinosaurs.

Dromaeosaur A carnivorous dinosaur, related to birds.

Fossil The remains of a prehistoric creature that has been preserved as a mould or cast in rock.

Frill Extra skin jutting out from the head, often supported by bone in ceratopsian dinosaurs.

Herbivore A plant-eating animal.

Hide The skin of a large animal, often thick and tough.

Jugular A large vein in the neck of an animal.

Jurassic A geological period following the Triassic and running from 200 to 145 million years ago. The climate was wetter than the Triassic with dinosaurs ruling the land, marine reptiles in the oceans and flying reptiles in the skies.

Omnivore An animal that eats both plants and meat.

Ornithiscians A set of plant-eating dinosaurs with hip bones that resemble those of modern birds (often called bird-hipped dinosaurs).

Peg-tooth A simple, slightly tapered tooth formation.

Piscivore A fish-eating animal.

Plumage The layer of feathers covering an animal.

Predator A hunting animal that feeds on other animals.

Prey An animal that is hunted and killed for food.

Glossary

Reptile A cold-blooded vertebrate animal with dry scaly skin that lays eggs on land. Modern reptiles include snakes, lizards, crocodiles, turtles and tortoises.

Saurischians A set of dinosaurs with hip bones that resemble those of modern reptiles (often called lizard-hipped dinosaurs). All carnivorous dinosaurs (theropods) were saurischians, as well as the plant-eating sauropods.

Sauropod An extremely large, saurischian, plant-eating dinosaur with a long neck, long tail and small head. They first appeared in the Late Triassic period.

Serrated Jagged-edged teeth and claws.

Sickle claw A large, curving hook-claw seen in the dromaeosaurid family, such as Deinonychus.

Thagomizer The spike-studded tail defence owned by stegosaurs (usually with four to ten spikes).

Theropod A bipedal carnivorous dinosaur with three-toed feet that appeared in the Late Triassic period. Includes many famous meat-eaters, such as Tyrannosaurus rex.

Tonne A unit of mass equal to 1000 kilograms.

Triassic A geological period following the Permian and running from 250 to 200 million years ago. The period was hot and dry and witnessed the rise and dominance of the dinosaurs.